W9-CIP-333

Fast Food

Sharon Dalgleish

Smart Apple Media

Smart Apple Media
2140 Howard Drive West
North Mankato
Minnesota 56003

First published in 2006 by
MACMILLAN EDUCATION AUSTRALIA PTY LTD
627 Chapel Street, South Yarra, Australia 3141

Visit our Web site at www.macmillan.com.au

Associated companies and representatives throughout the world.

Library of Congress Cataloging-in-Publication Data

Dalgleish, Sharon.
   Fast food / by Sharon Dalgleish.
      p. cm. – (Healthy choices)
   Includes index.
   ISBN-13: 978-1-58640-747-9
   1. Nutrition—Juvenile literature. 2. Convenience foods—Juvenile literature. 3. Quick and easy cookery—Juvenile literature. I. Title.

RA784.D337 2006
641.5'55—dc22

                                                                                    2005056806

Edited by Helen Bethune Moore
Text and cover design by Christine Deering
Page layout by Domenic Lauricella
Photo research by Legend Images
Illustrations by Paul Konye

Printed in USA

Acknowledgments
The author and the publisher are grateful to the following for permission to reproduce copyright material:

Front cover: Girls with healthy fast food, courtesy of Stockbyte.

Brand X Pictures, pp. 8, 18 (right), 19 (bottom left), 27 (left & bottom right); Corbis Digital Stock, pp. 18 (top left), 19 (top left), 23 (left), 27 (top right); Digital Vision, pp. 15 (bottom centre), 19 (top right); iStockphoto.com, pp. 1, 4 (left), 9 (top left & bottom), 14, 23 (top right); MEA Photo, p. 23 (bottom right); Photodisc, pp. 15 (left & top right), 18 (bottom left), 19 (bottom right), 22; Photolibrary/Foodpix, p. 3, 10, 11, 26; Photolibrary/Index Stock Imagery, p. 7; Photolibrary/Mauritius Die Bildagentur Gmbh, p. 9 (top right); Photolibrary/Plainpicture Gmbh & Co. Kg, pp. 4 (centre), 30; Photolibrary/Reso E.E.I.G, p. 4 (right); Stockbyte, p. 6.

While every care has been taken to trace and acknowledge copyright, the publisher tenders their apologies for any accidental infringement where copyright has proved untraceable. Where the attempt has been unsuccessful, the publisher welcomes information that would redress the situation.

Contents

Healthy, fit, and happy 4

Why make healthy choices? 6

Breakfast 8
Make granola 10
Make oatmeal 11
Make egg in a hole 12

More eggs 14
Make gooey egg bake 15
Make tomato scramble 16

Stir-fry 18
Make honey soy stir-fry 20

Pasta 22
Make macaroni cheese with a twist 23
Make chunky tomato sauce 24

Salads 26
Make a tossed salad 27
Make a salad bowl you can eat 28

Healthy choices for life 30

Glossary 31

Index 32

Healthy, fit, and happy

To be healthy, fit, and happy your body needs:

- a good mix of foods

- plenty of clean drinking water

- a **balance** of activity and rest

water

activity

A good mix of foods, water, rest, and play all help to make you healthy.

mix of foods

4

Fast food

The food group pyramid can help you make healthy choices when you need food fast.

grains   vegetables   fruits   oils   dairy foods   meat and beans

The food group pyramid shows you which foods to eat most for a healthy, balanced diet.

Why make healthy choices?

Making healthy choices is important, even when you are in a hurry. Most takeout foods are fast. However, they often have too much fat and salt, and not enough **fiber** or **nutrients**.

You can be really thirsty after eating takeout food because it is too salty.

Takeout food is fast, easy and there is no washing up. Many homemade choices are fast and easy, too. They can be healthier choices.

If you share the cleaning up it will quickly disappear.

Breakfast

A healthy breakfast gives you nutrients to help your body grow. Nutrients also help you think clearly. Even when you are in a hurry, make time for a healthy breakfast.

A fruit smoothie is a healthy and fast start to the day.

Eating different foods is interesting and fun, and gives your body lots of **vitamins**. Mix and match these healthy and fast ideas to try something new every day.

Try cereal with fruit instead of sugar.

Try banana, strawberries, blueberries, or canned fruit salad with yogurt.

Try toast with different toppings, such as baked beans, banana and ricotta cheese, or scrambled egg.

Make granola

You can make and store this granola so it is ready to go as fast as you are!

What you need
- 1 cup rolled oats
- 1 tablespoon unprocessed bran
- 2 tablespoons bran cereal
- 1 tablespoon wheat germ
- 2 tablespoons skim milk powder
- 1 tablespoon shredded coconut
- 3 tablespoons dried fruit, try cranberries, raisins, chopped apricots, chopped apple
- a mixing bowl
- a wooden spoon
- an airtight container

What to do
1. **Mix all the ingredients together in a bowl.**
2. **Store in an airtight container.**
3. **Serve two or three tablespoons of muesli in a bowl.**
4. **Spoon yogurt, or pour hot or cold milk, over the muesli.**

Make oatmeal

Ask a parent or teacher for help.

Oatmeal will fill you up on a cold morning and takes two minutes to cook.

Serves 1

What you need
- ¼ cup quick-cooking rolled oats
- ½ cup milk
- 1 tablespoon dried fruit bits
- a microwave-safe dish
- a wooden spoon
- a microwave oven
- extra milk (if you like)

What to do
1 Mix all ingredients in the microwave-safe dish.
2 Cover and cook in the microwave for 2 minutes.
3 Stir with a wooden spoon.
4 Serve with extra milk.

Make egg in a hole

This toast with an egg in the centre is perfect for a healthy breakfast in a hurry!

Serves 1

What you need
- 1 slice bread
- 1 tablespoon butter
- 1 egg
- a large cookie cutter
- a spatula
- a cup
- a frying pan

What to do

1 Use the cookie cutter to cut a shape in the middle of the bread.

2 Melt butter in a frying pan over medium heat. Place bread in pan and cook until bottom is golden. Turn over.

Ask a parent or teacher for help.

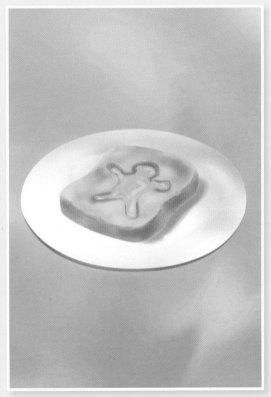

3 Crack the egg into a cup.

4 Pour egg into the cut-out shape. Cook for about 4 minutes until the egg is cooked.

More eggs

Eggs can be turned into a quick healthy meal any time. They contain **protein**, which your body needs. Eggs also contain **iron**. Iron helps your blood carry **oxygen**.

A hard-boiled egg is a quick way to get protein for your body.

Make gooey egg bake

Ask a parent or teacher for help.

These baked eggs are very quick and very easy. Serve them with a slice of whole grain toast.

Serves 1

What you need
- 1 slice lean ham, chopped
- ½ green onion, chopped finely
- 1 egg
- 1 tablespoon grated cheese
- a small ovenproof bowl, greased
- oven heated to 350 °F (180 °C)

What to do
1 **Put the ham and onion in the bottom of the bowl.**
2 **Break the egg on top.**
3 **Sprinkle cheese on top.**
4 **Bake for about 10 minutes.**

Make tomato scramble

The tomato in this scrambled egg gives you vitamins and fiber, as well as tasting great.

Serves 1

What you need

- 1 egg
- 1 tablespoon milk
- ½ medium tomato, chopped
- 1 slice bread, toasted
- 1 teaspoon butter or margarine
- sprig of parsley
- small mixing bowl
- a fork
- a frying pan
- a wooden spoon

What to do

1 **Break the egg into the bowl, then add the milk. Beat with the fork.**

2 **Add the chopped tomato and mix through.**

3 Melt the butter in a frying pan over medium heat. Pour the tomato and egg mixture into the frying pan.

4 Stir constantly until the mixture is a soft, creamy scramble. Serve with toast and decorate with parsley.

Stir-fry

Stir-frying is a fast and healthy way to cook vegetables. They stay crisp and crunchy, and they taste great. They also cook so quickly that they keep their vitamins.

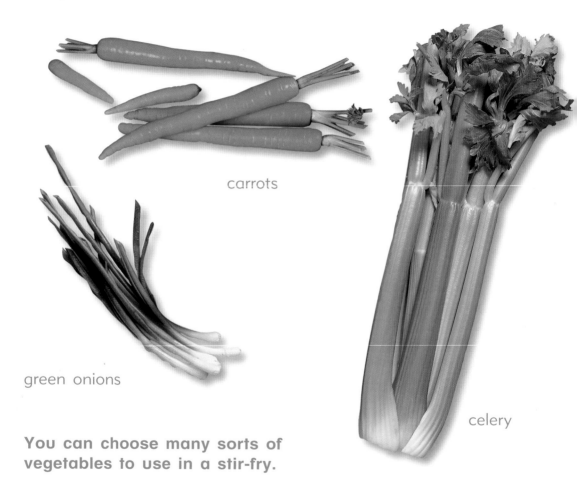

carrots

green onions

celery

You can choose many sorts of vegetables to use in a stir-fry.

Be prepared and have everything chopped and ready before you heat the wok. Once the preparation is done, your meal is almost ready!

peppers

cabbage

snow peas

meat

Slice the vegetables and meat into small pieces, so they will cook quickly.

Make honey soy stir-fry

It is easy to stir-fry a quick meal. You can change the recipe and use whatever vegetables you like. Leave out the chicken if you do not eat meat.

Serves 4

What you need

- 4 teaspoons vegetable oil
- 3 chicken breast fillets, sliced
- 1 carrot, sliced
- 3½ ounces (100 grams) snow peas, sliced
- ⅓ cup honey
- 2 teaspoons soy sauce
- cooked rice
- a wok or frying pan
- a wooden spoon

What to do

1 **Heat a wok or frying pan over high heat. Add half the oil.**

2 **Cook chicken in small batches for about 4 minutes. As each batch is cooked, set it aside on a plate.**

3 Add the rest of the oil to the wok. Add the hardest vegetables first as they take longest to cook. Stir-fry the vegetables for a minute or two.

4 Place the chicken back into the wok with the vegetables. Add the honey and soy sauce and cook for 1 minute, until the sauce thickens. Serve with rice.

Pasta

Pasta is made from different **grains**. Grain foods give you **energy**. Pasta cooks quickly so it is a good choice when you need energy in a hurry.

Pasta comes in different shapes, colors, and sizes.

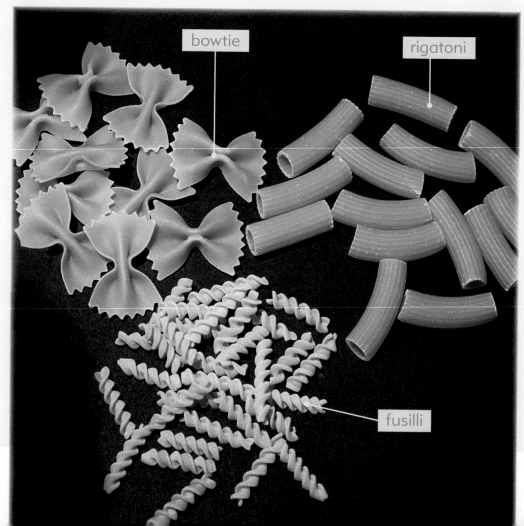

bowtie

rigatoni

fusilli

Make macaroni cheese with a twist

Ask a parent or teacher for help.

Tuna gives this quick and creamy pasta a twist of extra protein.

Serves 2

What you need

- 1½ cups macaroni
- ½ cup cream
- ½ cup grated cheese
- ½ cup tuna
- a large saucepan of water
- colander

cream

What to do

1 **Add the macaroni to a saucepan of boiling water. Cook for 6 minutes, or until just soft.**
2 **Drain the macaroni and put it back in the saucepan and cook on low heat.**
3 **Add the cream and cheese. Stir until the cheese melts.**
4 **Gently stir in the tuna and serve.**

Make chunky tomato sauce

This speedy spaghetti with sauce will fill you up and give you energy.

Serves 4

What you need

- 2 teaspoons vegetable oil
- 1 onion, chopped finely
- 4 ripe tomatoes, chopped finely
- 2 carrots, chopped
- 2 sticks of celery, chopped finely
- 2 tablespoons of tomato paste
- ½ cup of water

- pinch of sweet basil
- 14 ounces (400 grams) wheat spaghetti
- grated cheese
- a frying pan
- a wooden spoon
- a saucepan
- a strainer

What to do

1 **Heat the oil in the frying pan. Add the onion and fry until soft.**

2 **Stir in the tomato, carrots, celery, tomato paste, sweet basil, and water. Cover and simmer for about 15 minutes.**

Ask a parent or teacher for help.

3 Cook the spaghetti in a saucepan of boiling water until it is just soft. Strain the spaghetti.

4 Pour the sauce over the cooked spaghetti. Sprinkle with cheese.

Salads

Salads are a great way to eat a variety of vegetables at once. Vegetables contain fiber to help your body break down food. They also contain vitamins to help keep diseases away.

Serve a salad with any of the recipes in this book to make a healthy meal.

Make a tossed salad

This basic salad is quick and easy
to toss together.

Serves 2

What you need
- lettuce leaves, washed and dried
- spinach leaves, washed and dried
- 2 tomatoes, chopped
- 1 cucumber, sliced
- 2 oranges, peeled and sliced
- 1 boiled egg, sliced (if you like)
- a large bowl

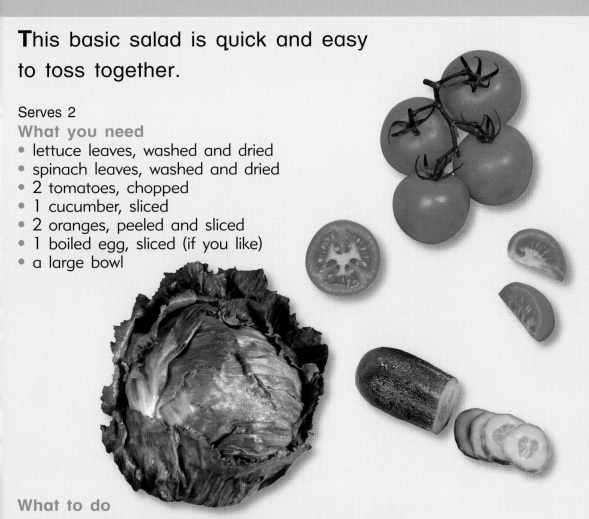

What to do
1 Put the first five ingredients in a large bowl.
2 Mix together.
3 If you are not eating any other protein foods, add the egg.
4 Serve and enjoy!

Make a salad bowl you can eat

This salad saves on washing up. When you have finished eating your vegetables, you can eat the bowl!

Serves 1 to 2

What you need

- 1 green, red, or yellow pepper, washed
- 1 stick celery, washed and cut into sticks
- 1 carrot, washed, peeled, and cut into sticks
- 8¾ ounce (250 gram) container of hummus
- a knife
- a spoon

What to do

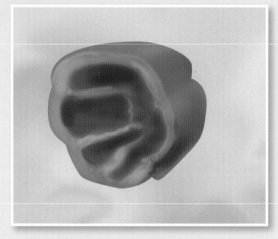

1 **Cut the pepper in half. Take out the seeds and white bits inside the pepper.**

2 **Spoon the hummus into the bottom of one half of the pepper.**

3 Cut the other half of the pepper into thin strips.

4 Arrange the vegetable sticks in the pepper bowl on top of the hummus. To eat, use the sticks to scoop out the hummus.

Healthy choices for life

Making healthy choices in everything you do will help you to be fit, happy, and healthy.

Life is fun when you make healthy choices.

Glossary

balance   an equal amount of different things

energy   strength to do things

fiber   found in plant foods, and helps your body break down food

grains   the hard seeds of cereals

iron   a mineral found in food that helps carry oxygen around your body

nutrients   healthy substances found in food, such as vitamins and minerals

oxygen   one of the gases in the air that people need to stay alive

protein   a substance found in food that builds muscles

vitamins   healthy substances found in food

Index

b
blood   14
breakfast   8

c
chunky tomato sauce   24–25

e
egg in a hole   12–13
eggs   14, 15, 16–17, 27

f
fiber   6, 16, 26
food group pyramid   4, 5
fruit   9, 10, 11
fruit and vegetable group   5

g
gooey egg bake   15
grain group   5, 22

i
iron   14

m
macaroni cheese with a
    twist   23
meat group   5
milk group   5
muesli   10

o
oxygen   14

p
pasta   22, 23, 24–25
porridge   11
protein   14, 23, 27

r
recipes   10, 11, 12–13, 15,
    16–17, 20–21, 23, 24–25,
    27, 28–29

s
salads   26, 27, 28, 29
salt   6
smoothie   8
stir-fry   18, 19, 20–21

t
takeout foods   6, 7
toast   9, 15, 17

v
vegetables   18, 19, 20, 21, 28,
    29
vitamins   9, 16, 18, 26